"My Colt"

The Story of Traveller, Robert E. Lee's Famous Warhorse

By Margaret Samdahl

Margaret Samdahl

Illustrated by Carol Blair

C. J. BLAIR

First Edition: February, 2018
Printed in the United States of America
ISBN: 978-0-9994689-4-4

To Gin—

for her constant encouragement in writing this story.

Acknowledgements

Thank you to Jessica Bowers of Washington and Lee University's Lee Chapel for her enthusiasm and ideas for this book.

Thank you to my husband, Don Samdahl, for his technical expertise which made printing this story possible.

Last, but not least, many thanks to Carol Blair whose artwork has made Traveller's story come alive.

Carol Blair and I would like to thank Lisa McCown, Byron Faidley, Seth McCormick-Goodhart, and Tom Camden of Washington and Lee University's Special Collections and Archives for their help with letters, articles, and details related to Traveller and his story.

Growing Up on the Farm
Greenbrier County: 1857

Two things you should know about me from the beginning. The first is my name was not always Traveller. The second is I did not know I would grow up to become a famous warhorse.

My life began in the misty mountains in western Virginia. I was a steel gray colt with a black mane and tail and everyone said I was beautiful. I lived on a farm with large green pastures and loved to gallop up and down the mountains with the other horses. The owner of the farm, Mr. Andrew Johnston, was a nice and kind man. He gave me the name Jeff Davis. Who was that? I was told Jefferson Davis was a senator who became the United States Secretary of War. That sounded very important to me. I would have to work hard to live up to such a name.

My Early Life: 1858—1860

Each year I grew taller and stronger. Galloping up and down the mountains in the pasture gave me powerful muscles and, like my father, I was a fast runner. He was a well-known racehorse who was named Grey Eagle. My mother, Flora, had encouraged me to remember my name, Jeff Davis, so I wanted to do something important and be noticed. My first chance was at the County Fair. It was so exciting to travel to county seat for the fair, but I tried my best to be well behaved. You may not believe it, but as a young and spirited horse, this was difficult. I must have succeeded, however, for the judges awarded me first prize two years in a row! My mother was very proud of me.

The War Begins: 1861

My peaceful and fun life on the Johnston farm ended in 1861. War had begun. The men fighting in the war were called soldiers. Some soldiers walked. They were known as the infantry. Others rode horses to battle. They were the cavalry.

I was sold to two brothers who were soldiers. Their names were Thomas and Joseph Broun. They needed a strong and brave warhorse. I was certain I could trot and gallop for long distances and I knew I was brave. I was just the horse a soldier needed. The Brouns were wonderful owners. They were proud to ride me, take care of me, and best of all, to pat me often.

At this time, I was also called Greenbrier. This was the name of the county where I was born. How important to have another name! I was called Jeff by Joseph Broun and Greenbrier by others. This did not bother me (I was a smart horse) and Greenbrier reminded me of home.

Meeting Robert E. Lee: 1861

One day, Joseph Broun and I were riding in the mountains to meet the leaders of the local soldiers. It was a chilly autumn day. I was full of energy and we cantered up the mountainside. The path was blocked and I had to jump over the obstacle to reach the group of men at the campfire. When we arrived, an older soldier walked over to pat me. He seemed to be in charge. I was told his name was General Robert E. Lee. He asked my owner if there were other Greenbrier horses just like me? What a question! I knew none compared to me!

I pranced around the campfire as the soldiers admired me. Joseph Broun told General Lee I was not for sale. Nevertheless, the general called me "my colt." This was strange to me for I still belonged to the Broun brothers. For the first time, I thought, was I becoming famous? So many compliments on my stamina, courage, and beauty can give a horse a big head.

A New Owner and a New Name: 1861—1862

Warhorses and soldiers have to travel. We packed up to travel to South Carolina. I had never been so far from home and I missed the mountains, the cool air, and my barnyard friends.

While in South Carolina, we saw General Lee. Again, he talked to my owner, Joseph Broun, patted me on the head, and called me “my colt”. I really liked him.

For two weeks, Robert E. Lee rode me every day and we became friends, marching far and wide. He was a skilled horseman and it was fun to be with him. I was told what a wonderful horse I was. The next time I saw Joseph Broun, he was handed two one-hundred-dollar Confederate bills to pay for me. I had a new owner, Robert E Lee. He gave me the name Traveller.

Jeff Davis, Greenbrier, My Colt, and now Traveller—four names in the four years of my life—could that be a record breaker? My original namesake, Jefferson Davis, is now president of the Confederate States of America. He has made the history books. I wonder if I will?

Greenbrier, the name of the county where I was born, would soon become a county in West Virginia when it became a state. So many events are happening. Little did I know the many miles General Lee and I would travel together over the next years. We were marching into history.

War Time: 1862—1865

I soon discovered being a warhorse can be difficult. Bullets and cannonballs flying through the air are scary. And the noise! The sound of battle was worse than any thunderstorm and the smoke, smell, and confusion were frightening.

My new owner, General Lee, was fearless. With him, I was not afraid in the battles even though we were always in the midst of great action. Men, horses, and equipment were on the move. We often marched night and day but I was young and high-spirited. Marching was fine with me.

General Lee often had to review his troops. This was one of my most enjoyable activities. While the general owned other warhorses, I was his favorite, and he selected me from his horses for the reviews. We would gallop with other horsemen for miles to see the soldiers lined up for inspection. One time, the review was nine miles.

The horses and riders in our escort could not keep up with General Lee and me as the men cheered when we thundered by. I have never been prouder of myself and my new owner. We had become constant companions and best friends.

But war was not fun. Many days there was not enough food for the horses or the men. I dreamed of the green pastures of my childhood and hoped the war would end soon.

The War Ends
Appomattox, Virginia: 1865

Four years I have been a warhorse in the Civil War. It seems much longer. This spring, April 1865, I sensed a change. The weary men and their mounts marched much slower. Even my master seemed different. There was much talk of no supplies and whether we could get them from the train. I did not understand.

One day, General Lee had me saddled and said we had to go to a place called Appomattox. He spoke quietly to me but seemed very sad. I pranced and tossed my head as we rode to Appomattox. The men along the road cheered and saluted, but my master did not smile. As we approached the meeting place, I saw a group of men. I did not recognize them or their horses. They were Union soldiers. I trotted boldly to the area as a famous warhorse should. An attendant took my reins and General Lee walked up the steps and entered the house. When he returned we slowly rode away and headed to Richmond. The soldiers who lined the paths all lifted their hats in respect. General Lee nodded in their direction as we turned away. We shared a quiet moment together by a creek where I took a much needed drink of water. I learned a surrender had been signed. The war was over.

After the War: 1865

In Richmond, Virginia I was hugged and patted by many people. But I missed the days of riding and the constant companionship of my owner Robert E. Lee. It was lonely being in a stable and not a few steps away from General Lee, my very best friend. I think he tired of the noise and crowds in Richmond too.

Soon we were heading out of town. We rode west for many miles into the country to Derwent Cottage. A nice friend of the Lee family suggested we retire to this quiet place. The house was small, but the pasture was large with plenty of room to roam. It reminded me of my childhood and I was content there. I noticed my friend's gray military coat no longer had the decorations on it and the buttons had been changed. It was just plain gray and matched the color of my hair. The steel gray coat of my youth had changed to a Confederate gray color as I became older.

At Derwent, we rode for hours every day along the country roads. It was a happy time for us. One day a stranger came to our remote cottage. He stayed a while and then departed. After this meeting, my owner appeared to be lost in thought. Before too long he patted my neck and told me we were taking a trip. We packed up and headed to Lexington, Virginia. It was just the two of us and like old times when we traveled far and wide together.

Carol Blair

A New Job: 1865—1870

We rode west for days and each day I became more excited. The mountains were in sight! Could we be returning to my childhood home? But no, we finally stopped in the sleepy little town of Lexington, Virginia. I heard we were only seventy miles from the Johnston farm where I was born. While Lexington was not my birthplace, it was close enough. There were hills and valleys and cool air to breathe.

The children brought me flowers in garlands to put around my neck. I'm certain I looked very handsome, but for me, the flowers were best to eat. I was honored not only with flowers but with a photograph. The photographer, Mr. Michael Miley of Lexington, told me to stand very still and not even swish my tail!

I liked flowers, and photographs were acceptable, but being famous can be unpleasant too. My mane and tail were being plucked. One young man said, “Thanks Traveller for the memento” as he grabbed a fist full of my mane and pulled it out. What is a memento? I am not certain. I only know I had less hair! To make it even more embarrassing, General Lee told his friends I looked like a plucked chicken. But I discovered I could prance in place and keep the pluckers away. A brave and famous warhorse must have a full mane and tail! In Lexington, I had a new job too. I was the mount for a president. General Lee was now president of Washington College.

Our Final Home: 1865—1870

The war was over and battlefields a thing of the past. Instead of living in a tent or under the starry sky, we now had a real home. The house was on the grounds of Washington College in the little town of Lexington, Virginia. My owner and I even lived under the same roof. My stable was connected by a breezeway to the house!

Every day after his busy schedule as college president, we would ride out from town. My owner and friend realized we both needed to relax. We loved to thunder up and down mountain paths and jump creeks. To keep busy while my companion was at work, I would graze in the family's front yard. They lived in a large house with a wide porch. Often the Lee family and friends would sit on the porch and talk to me. I would amble over to the railing and be fed a delicious sugar cube. They would pat me too. I have to say I did not miss the bullets, bombs, or confusion of the war. This quiet life suited me just fine.

Each year in Lexington I noticed that our hair was getting whiter. My master's beard and hair were turning snowy white. My beautiful Confederate gray coat was fading too. I did not feel any older and could still trot and canter for quite a way. But my companion seemed to tire easily and would slow me to a walk. Our rides became shorter and we did not travel too far. I tried to be as gentle as possible as we trotted along. It was my time to take care of my master. It was my job to go slowly and be patient as he had been with me all these years.

When the time came that we could no longer travel up and down the mountains roads, we continued to be together. He would whistle for me from the front porch and I would happily come to visit him and we would enjoy each other's company. We would remain best friends for the rest of our lives.

Glossary

Civil War—in America, a war fought between the states from 1861-1865.

Confederacy—the Confederate States of American (CSA) was a group of Southern states which left the Union and fought against states that remained in the Union in the American Civil War.

Garland—a wreath or rope of flowers.

Gaits of a horse: walk, trot, canter, and gallop.

Greenbrier County—an area on the boundary of the states Virginia and West Virginia. At Traveller's birth, it was part of Virginia. It is now in the state of West Virginia.

Jefferson Davis—a well-known American Democratic politician. He was a member of the United States Congress from Mississippi, the United States Secretary of War, 1853- 1857, and from 1861-1865, President of the Confederacy.

Memento—something that reminds one of past events—a souvenir.

Union—mostly northern states remained in the Union and fought against the South in the American Civil War.

Afternote

There are different stories of how Robert E. Lee and Traveller met in 1861 in the hills of western Virginia. For *My Colt*, Joseph Broun's memories of the event were used from a letter he wrote March 9, 1904, to his niece, Miss Martha Knott Ordway.

Robert E. Lee died October 12, 1870, and is buried inside Lee Chapel on the campus of Washington and Lee University in Lexington, Virginia. Traveller died one year later and is buried outside Lee Chapel. As in life, Traveller remains only a few feet away from his friend and constant companion, Robert E. Lee.

Made in the USA
Middletown, DE
08 September 2021